SECURE
THE THIRTY-ONE DAY PRAYER JOURNAL

CONNECTING TO GOD THROUGH PERSISTENT PRAYER

SUSANNAH BAKER

LUCIDBOOKS

Secure: The Thirty-One Day Prayer Journal
Connecting to God Through Persistent Prayer

Copyright © 2018 by Susannah Baker

Published by Lucid Books in Houston, TX
www.LucidBooksPublishing.com

All rights reserved. No part of this publication may be reproduced, stored in a retrieval system, or transmitted in any form by any means, electronic, mechanical, photocopy, recording, or otherwise, without the prior permission of the publisher, except as provided for by USA copyright law.

All rights reserved. No part of this publication may be reproduced, stored in a retrieval system, or transmitted in any form by any means, electronic, mechanical, photocopy, recording, or otherwise, without the prior permission of the publisher, except as provided for by USA copyright law.

ISBN-10: 1-63296-240-3
ISBN-13: 978-1-63296-240-9
eISBN-10: 1-63296-241-1
eISBN-13: 978-1-63296-241-6

Special Sales: Most Lucid Books titles are available in special quantity discounts. Custom imprinting or excerpting can also be done to fit special needs. Contact Lucid Books at info@lucidbookspublishing.com.

SECURE
THE THIRTY-ONE DAY PRAYER JOURNAL

Table of Contents

How to Use this Prayer Journal	1
Day One	4
Day Two	6
Day Three	8
Day Four	10
Day Five	12
Day Six	14
Day Seven	16
Day Eight	18
Day Nine	20
Day Ten	22
Day Eleven	24
Day Twelve	26
Day Thirteen	28
Day Fourteen	30
Day Fifteen	32
Day Sixteen	34
Day Seventeen	36
Day Eighteen	38
Day Nineteen	40
Day Twenty	42
Day Twenty-One	44
Day Twenty-Two	46
Day Twenty-Three	48

Day Twenty-Four	50
Day Twenty-Five	52
Day Twenty-Six	54
Day Twenty-Seven	56
Day Twenty-Eight	58
Day Twenty-Nine	60
Day Thirty	62
Day Thirty-One	64

How to Use This Prayer Journal

In Luke 11:5–13, Jesus told us to pray persistently because persistent prayer is a discipline that attaches our souls to a good father who loves to give the good gift of His presence and spirit to His children each and every time we ask Him. That is why learning to pray persistently isn't just a suggestion; it is essential for life as children of God. As beloved children, persistent prayer changes how we understand, live out, and tell our stories. But most importantly, it allows us to attach securely to our heavenly father and see the circumstances of our lives through the lens of a good father who never leaves or forsakes us but loves us with an everlasting love and works out all things for our good.

As important as persistent prayer is, I have found that when I set aside time to pray, unless I have some sort of structure or system in place, I end up being so overwhelmed by all the things I could pray for that I end up praying at a very shallow level or not praying at all. I have also found that the more complicated I try to make my prayer life, the less I pray.

To help with both problems, I created a simple prayer guide, *Secure: Connecting to God Through Persistent Prayer*, and this journal to help you work through the guide for 31 days.

I found that with the prayer guide in one hand and a blank journal in the other, the rhythm of prayer was often difficult to begin or maintain, especially during busy or difficult seasons of life. But by putting a few simple prompts in place using the acronym PRAY—Praise, Repent, Ask, and Yield—my prayers began to flow with much more ease and consistency.

Each of the 31 days of this journal has space for you to write down your prayers of Praise, Repentance, Asking, and Yielding, following the format in the prayer guide. And once you are finished with the 31 days, you can continue your habit of prayer using the same prompts in a journal of your choice.

If there are days you want or need to spend all your time in just one section rather than all four, feel free to do so. My hope in offering this journal is not to put rigid rules in place that you feel you have to follow, but to provide simple prompts through which the Holy Spirit can move at His pace and on His timetable in your life.

Don't wait to start the prayer journal until you have the perfect amount of time or are in the perfect season of life. Just begin to pray wherever you are in whatever season of life you are in, knowing that your times of persistent prayer in God's word will securely connect you to God in a way that heals your soul, changes your story, and transforms the world.

For videos and further resources in learning how to securely attach and connect to your Heavenly Father, visit www.susannahbaker.com.

Day One

Praise:

Read Psalm 8:1–9 and make the psalmist's story your own, incorporating the words into your own prayer of praise.

_____
_____
_____
_____
_____

Repent:

Turn to the Repentance section in your prayer guide. Write a prayer of repentance for any sin from the day you need to confess and a prayer of forgiveness for those you need to forgive on a one-time or ongoing basis.

_____
_____
_____
_____

Ask:

Turn to the appropriate day of the week in the Ask section of your prayer guide. Write a prayer for the topic you have chosen at the top of your page, using scripture to guide you in your prayer. (To find scripture to help you pray, use the tools at the back of the Ask section.)

_____

_____

_____

_____

_____

Yield:

Turn to the Yield section in your prayer guide and write a prayer of surrender for the day, releasing your worries and anxieties and securely attaching yourself to the presence, power, and love of the Lord for all that lies ahead.

_____

_____

_____

_____

_____

Day Two

Praise:

Read Psalm 9:1–10 and make the psalmist's story your own, incorporating the words into your own prayer of praise.

_____

_____

_____

_____

Repent:

Turn to the Repentance section in your prayer guide. Write a prayer of repentance for any sin from the day you need to confess and a prayer of repentance for anyone from whom you need to ask for forgiveness. With the Lord's leading, make a plan to repent to whomever you have sinned against.

_____

_____

_____

_____

Ask:

Turn to the appropriate day of the week in the Ask section of your prayer guide. Write a prayer for the topic you have chosen at the top of your page, using scripture to guide you in your prayer. (To find scripture to help you pray, use the tools at the back of the Ask section.)

_____

_____

_____

_____

_____

Yield:

Turn to the Yield section in your prayer guide and write a prayer of surrender for the day, releasing your worries and anxieties and securely attaching yourself to the presence, power, and love of the Lord for all that lies ahead.

_____

_____

_____

_____

Day Three

Praise:

Read Psalm 16:5–11 and make the psalmist's story your own, incorporating the words into your own prayer of praise.

_____

_____

_____

_____

_____

Repent:

Turn to the Repentance section in your prayer guide. Write a prayer of repentance for any sin from the day that you need to confess and a prayer confessing areas of sin and temptation with which you struggle habitually. Ask the Lord to help you guard against these sins and begin to walk out of destructive life patterns.

_____

_____

_____

_____

_____

Ask:

Turn to the appropriate day of the week in the Ask section of your prayer guide. Write a prayer for the topic you have chosen at the top of your page, using scripture to guide you in your prayers. (To find scripture to help you pray, use the tools at the back of the Ask section.)

_____

_____

_____

_____

_____

Yield:

Turn to the Yield section in your prayer guide and write a prayer of surrender for the day, releasing your worries and anxieties and securely attaching yourself to the presence, power, and love of the Lord for all that lies ahead.

_____

_____

_____

_____

Day Four

Praise:

Read Psalm 19:1–14 and make the psalmist's story your own, incorporating the words into your own prayer of praise.

_____

_____

_____

_____

_____

Repent:

Turn to the Repentance section in your prayer guide. Write a prayer of repentance for any sin from the day that you need to confess and a prayer asking for the wisdom, accountability, and humility to see areas of past deception and temptation that could surface again and cause you to stumble and fall in the future.

_____

_____

_____

_____

_____

Ask:

Turn to the appropriate day of the week in the Ask section of your prayer guide. Write a prayer for the topic you have chosen at the top of your page, using scripture to guide you in your prayers. (To find scripture to help you pray, use the tools at the back of the Ask section.)

_____

_____

_____

_____

_____

Yield:

Turn to the Yield section in your prayer guide and write a prayer of surrender for the day, releasing your worries and anxieties and securely attaching yourself to the presence, power, and love of the Lord for all that lies ahead.

_____

_____

_____

_____

Day Five

Praise:

Read Psalm 29:1–11 and make the psalmist's story your own, incorporating the words into your own prayer of praise.

_____

_____

_____

_____

_____

Repent:

Turn to the Repentance section in your prayer guide. Write a prayer of repentance for any sin from the day that you need to confess, and then take time to pray through and receive God's forgiveness and covering love in the areas you need them the most.

_____

_____

_____

_____

_____

Ask:

Turn to the appropriate day of the week in the Ask section of your prayer guide. Write a prayer for the topic you have chosen at the top of your page, using scripture to guide you in your prayers. (To find scripture to help you pray, use the tools at the back of the Ask section.)

_____

_____

_____

_____

_____

Yield:

Turn to the Yield section in your prayer guide and write a prayer of surrender for the day, releasing your worries and anxieties and securely attaching yourself to the presence, power, and love of the Lord for all that lies ahead.

_____

_____

_____

_____

_____

Day Six

Praise:

Read Psalm 33:1–12 and make the psalmist's story your own, incorporating the words into your own prayer of praise.

_____

_____

_____

_____

Repent:

Turn to the Repentance section in your prayer guide. Write a prayer of repentance for any sin from the day that you need to confess and a prayer of forgiveness for those you need to forgive on a one-time or ongoing basis.

_____

_____

_____

_____

Ask:

Turn to the appropriate day of the week in the Ask section of your prayer guide. Write a prayer for the topic you have chosen at the top of your page, using scripture to guide you in your prayers. (To find scripture to help you pray, use the tools at the back of the Ask section.)

_____

_____

_____

_____

_____

Yield:

Turn to the Yield section in your prayer guide and write a prayer of surrender for the day, releasing your worries and anxieties and securely attaching yourself to the presence, power, and love of the Lord for all that lies ahead.

_____

_____

_____

_____

_____

Day Seven

Praise:

Read Psalm 47:1–9 and make the psalmist's story your own, incorporating the words into your own prayer of praise.

_____

_____

_____

_____

_____

Repent:

Turn to the Repentance section in your prayer guide. Write a prayer of repentance for any sin from the day that you need to confess and a prayer of repentance for anyone from whom you need to ask for forgiveness. With the Lord's leading, make a plan to repent to whomever it is you have sinned against.

_____

_____

_____

_____

Ask:

Turn to the appropriate day of the week in the Ask section of your prayer guide. Write a prayer for the topic you have chosen at the top of your page, using scripture to guide you in your prayers. (To find scripture to help you pray, use the tools at the back of the Ask section.)

_____

_____

_____

_____

_____

Yield:

Turn to the Yield section in your prayer guide and write a prayer of surrender for the day, releasing your worries and anxieties and securely attaching yourself to the presence, power, and love of the Lord for all that lies ahead.

_____

_____

_____

_____

_____

Day Eight

Praise:

Read Psalm 48:1–14 and make the psalmist's story your own, incorporating the words into your own prayer of praise.

_____

_____

_____

_____

_____

Repent:

Turn to the Repentance section in your prayer guide. Write a prayer of repentance for any sin from the day that you need to confess and a prayer confessing areas of sin and temptation with which you struggle habitually. Ask the Lord to help you guard against these sins and begin to walk out of destructive life patterns.

_____

_____

_____

_____

_____

Ask:

Turn to the appropriate day of the week in the Ask section of your prayer guide. Write a prayer for the topic you have chosen at the top of your page, using scripture to guide you in your prayers. (To find scripture to help you pray, use the tools at the back of the Ask section.)

_____

_____

_____

_____

_____

Yield:

Turn to the Yield section in your prayer guide and write a prayer of surrender for the day, releasing your worries and anxieties and securely attaching yourself to the presence, power, and love of the Lord for all that lies ahead.

_____

_____

_____

_____

Day Nine

Praise:

Read Psalm 63:1–11 and make the psalmist's story your own, incorporating the words into your own prayer of praise.

_____

_____

_____

_____

_____

Repent:

Turn to the Repentance section in your prayer guide. Write a prayer of repentance for any sin from the day you need to confess and a prayer asking for the wisdom, accountability, and humility to see areas of past deception and temptation that could surface again and cause you to stumble and fall in the future.

_____

_____

_____

_____

_____

Ask:

Turn to the appropriate day of the week in the ask section of your prayer guide. Write a prayer for the topic you have chosen at the top of your page, using scripture to guide you in your prayers. (To find scripture to help you pray, use the tools at the back of the ask section.)

_____

_____

_____

_____

Yield:

Turn to the Yield section in your prayer guide and write a prayer of surrender for the day, releasing your worries and anxieties and securely attaching yourself to the presence, power, and love of the Lord for all that lies ahead.

_____

_____

_____

_____

Day Ten

Praise:

Read Psalm 66:1-20 and make the psalmist's story your own, incorporating his words into your own prayer of praise.

_____

_____

_____

_____

_____

Repent:

Turn to the Repentance section in your prayer guide. Write a prayer of repentance for any sin from the day you need to confess, and then take time to pray through and receive God's forgiveness and covering love in the areas you need it the most.

_____

_____

_____

_____

_____

Ask:

Turn to the appropriate day of the week in the Ask section of your prayer guide. Write a prayer for the topic you have chosen at the top of your page, using scripture to guide you in your prayers. (To find scripture to help you pray, use the tools at the back of the Ask section.)

_____

_____

_____

_____

_____

Yield:

Turn to the Yield section in your prayer guide and write a prayer of surrender for the day, releasing your worries and anxieties and securely attaching yourself to the presence, power, and love of the Lord for all that lies ahead.

_____

_____

_____

_____

Day Eleven

Praise:

Read Psalm 67:1–7 and make the psalmist's story your own, incorporating the words into your own prayer of praise.

_____

_____

_____

_____

_____

Repent:

Turn to the Repentance section in your prayer guide. Write a prayer of repentance for any sin from the day that you need to confess and a prayer of forgiveness for those you need to forgive on a one-time or ongoing basis.

_____

_____

_____

_____

_____

Ask:

Turn to the appropriate day of the week in the Ask section of your prayer guide. Write a prayer for the topic you have chosen at the top of your page, using scripture to guide you in your prayers. (To find scripture to help you pray, use the tools at the back of the Ask section.)

_____

_____

_____

_____

_____

Yield:

Turn to the Yield section in your prayer guide and write a prayer of surrender for the day, releasing your worries and anxieties and securely attaching yourself to the presence, power, and love of the Lord for all that lies ahead.

_____

_____

_____

_____

_____

Day Twelve

Praise:

Read Psalm 75:1–10 and make the psalmist's story your own, incorporating the words into your own prayer of praise.

Repent:

Turn to the Repentance section in your prayer guide. Write a prayer of repentance for any sin from the day that you need to confess and a prayer of repentance for anyone from whom you need to ask for forgiveness. With the Lord's leading, make a plan to repent to whomever it is you have sinned against.

Ask:

Turn to the appropriate day of the week in the Ask section of your prayer guide. Write a prayer for the topic you have chosen at the top of your page, using scripture to guide you in your prayers. (To find scripture to help you pray, use the tools at the back of the Ask section.)

_____

_____

_____

_____

Yield:

Turn to the Yield section in your prayer guide and write a prayer of surrender for the day, releasing your worries and anxieties and securely attaching yourself to the presence, power, and love of the Lord for all that lies ahead.

_____

_____

_____

_____

Day Thirteen

Praise:

Read Psalm 81:1–16 and make the psalmist's story your own, incorporating the words into your own prayer of praise.

_____

_____

_____

_____

Repent:

Turn to the Repentance section in your prayer guide. Write a prayer of repentance for any sin from the day that you need to confess and a prayer confessing areas of sin and temptation with which you struggle habitually. Ask the Lord to help you guard against these sins and begin to walk out of destructive life patterns.

_____

_____

_____

_____

Ask:

Turn to the appropriate day of the week in the Ask section of your prayer guide. Write a prayer for the topic you have chosen at the top of your page, using scripture to guide you in your prayers. (To find scripture to help you pray, use the tools at the back of the Ask section.)

_____

_____

_____

_____

_____

Yield:

Turn to the Yield section in your prayer guide and write a prayer of surrender for the day, releasing your worries and anxieties and securely attaching yourself to the presence, power, and love of the Lord for all that lies ahead.

_____

_____

_____

_____

_____

Day Fourteen

Praise:

Read Psalm 84:1–12 and make the psalmist's story your own, incorporating the words into your own prayer of praise.

_____

_____

_____

_____

_____

Repent:

Turn to the Repentance section in your prayer guide. Write a prayer of repentance for any sin from the day that you need to confess and a prayer asking for the wisdom, accountability, and humility to see areas of past deception and temptation that could surface again and cause you to stumble and fall in the future.

_____

_____

_____

_____

_____

Ask:

Turn to the appropriate day of the week in the Ask section of your prayer guide. Write a prayer for the topic you have chosen at the top of your page, using scripture to guide you in your prayers. (To find scripture to help you pray, use the tools at the back of the Ask section.)

_____

_____

_____

_____

_____

Yield:

Turn to the Yield section in your prayer guide and write a prayer of surrender for the day, releasing your worries and anxieties and securely attaching yourself to the presence, power, and love of the Lord for all that lies ahead.

_____

_____

_____

_____

_____

Day Fifteen

Praise:

Read Psalm 92:1–9 and make the psalmist's story your own, incorporating the words into your own prayer of praise.

_____
_____
_____
_____

Repent:

Turn to the Repentance section in your prayer guide. Write a prayer of repentance for any sin from the day you need to confess, and then take time to pray through and receive God's forgiveness and covering love in the areas you need it the most.

_____
_____
_____
_____

Ask:

Turn to the appropriate day of the week in the Ask section of your prayer guide. Write a prayer for the topic you have chosen at the top of your page, using scripture to guide you in your prayers. (To find scripture to help you pray, use the tools at the back of the Ask section.)

_____

_____

_____

_____

_____

Yield:

Turn to the Yield section in your prayer guide and write a prayer of surrender for the day, releasing your worries and anxieties and securely attaching yourself to the presence, power, and love of the Lord for all that lies ahead.

_____

_____

_____

_____

_____

Day Sixteen

Praise:

Read Psalm 95:1–11 and make the psalmist's story your own, incorporating the words into your own prayer of praise.

_____
_____
_____
_____

Repent:

Turn to the Repentance section in your prayer guide. Write a prayer of repentance for any sin from the day that you need to confess and a prayer of forgiveness for those you need to forgive on a one-time or ongoing basis.

_____
_____
_____
_____

Ask:

Turn to the appropriate day of the week in the Ask section of your prayer guide. Write a prayer for the topic you have chosen at the top of your page, using scripture to guide you in your prayers. (To find scripture to help you pray, use the tools at the back of the Ask section.)

_____

_____

_____

_____

_____

Yield:

Turn to the Yield section in your prayer guide and write a prayer of surrender for the day, releasing your worries and anxieties and securely attaching yourself to the presence, power, and love of the Lord for all that lies ahead.

_____

_____

_____

_____

_____

Day Seventeen

Praise:

Read Psalm 96:1–13 and make the psalmist's story your own, incorporating the words into your own prayer of praise.

_____

_____

_____

_____

Repent:

Turn to the Repentance section in your prayer guide. Write a prayer of repentance for any sin from the day that you need to confess and a prayer of repentance for anyone from whom you need to ask for forgiveness. With the Lord's leading, make a plan to repent to whomever it is you have sinned against.

_____

_____

_____

_____

Ask:

Turn to the appropriate day of the week in the Ask section of your prayer guide. Write a prayer for the topic you have chosen at the top of your page, using scripture to guide you in your prayers. (To find scripture to help you pray, use the tools at the back of the Ask section.)

_____

_____

_____

_____

_____

Yield:

Turn to the Yield section in your prayer guide and write a prayer of surrender for the day, releasing your worries and anxieties and securely attaching yourself to the presence, power, and love of the Lord for all that lies ahead.

_____

_____

_____

_____

_____

Day Eighteen

Praise:

Read Psalm 98:1–9 and make the psalmist's story your own, incorporating the words into your own prayer of praise.

Repent:

Turn to the Repentance section in your prayer guide. Write a prayer of repentance for any sin from the day that you need to confess and a prayer confessing areas of sin and temptation with which you struggle habitually. Ask the Lord to help you guard against these sins and begin to walk out of destructive life patterns.

Ask:

Turn to the appropriate day of the week in the Ask section of your prayer guide. Write a prayer for the topic you have chosen at the top of your page, using scripture to guide you in your prayers. (To find scripture to help you pray, use the tools at the back of the Ask section.)

_____

_____

_____

_____

_____

Yield:

Turn to the Yield section in your prayer guide and write a prayer of surrender for the day, releasing your worries and anxieties and securely attaching yourself to the presence, power, and love of the Lord for all that lies ahead.

_____

_____

_____

_____

_____

Day Nineteen

Praise:

Read Psalm 99:1–9 and make the psalmist's story your own, incorporating the words into your own prayer of praise.

Repent:

Turn to the Repentance section in your prayer guide. Write a prayer of repentance for any sin from the day that you need to confess and a prayer asking for the wisdom, accountability, and humility to see areas of past deception and temptation that could surface again and cause you to stumble and fall in the future.

Ask:

Turn to the appropriate day of the week in the Ask section of your prayer guide. Write a prayer for the topic you have chosen at the top of your page, using scripture to guide you in your prayers. (To find scripture to help you pray, use the tools at the back of the Ask section.)

_____

_____

_____

_____

_____

Yield:

Turn to the Yield section in your prayer guide and write a prayer of surrender for the day, releasing your worries and anxieties and securely attaching yourself to the presence, power, and love of the Lord for all that lies ahead.

_____

_____

_____

_____

_____

Day Twenty

Praise:

Read Psalm 100:1–5 and make the psalmist's story your own, incorporating the words into your own prayer of praise.

_____

_____

_____

_____

Repent:

Turn to the Repentance section in your prayer guide. Write a prayer of repentance for any sin from the day you need to confess, and then take time to pray through and receive God's forgiveness and covering love in the areas you need it the most.

_____

_____

_____

_____

Ask:

Turn to the appropriate day of the week in the Ask section of your prayer guide. Write a prayer for the topic you have chosen at the top of your page, using scripture to guide you in your prayers. (To find scripture to help you pray, use the tools at the back of the Ask section.)

_____

_____

_____

_____

_____

Yield:

Turn to the Yield section in your prayer guide and write a prayer of surrender for the day, releasing your worries and anxieties and securely attaching yourself to the presence, power, and love of the Lord for all that lies ahead.

_____

_____

_____

_____

_____

Day Twenty-One

Praise:

Read Psalm 103:1–22 and make the psalmist's story your own, incorporating the words into your own prayer of praise.

_____

_____

_____

_____

Repent:

Turn to the Repentance section in your prayer guide. Write a prayer of repentance for any sin from the day that you need to confess and a prayer of forgiveness for those you need to forgive on a one-time or ongoing basis.

_____

_____

_____

_____

Ask:

Turn to the appropriate day of the week in the Ask section of your prayer guide. Write a prayer for the topic you have chosen at the top of your page, using scripture to guide you in your prayers. (To find scripture to help you pray, use the tools at the back of the Ask section.)

_____

_____

_____

_____

Yield:

Turn to the Yield section in your prayer guide and write a prayer of surrender for the day, releasing your worries and anxieties and securely attaching yourself to the presence, power, and love of the Lord for all that lies ahead.

_____

_____

_____

_____

Day Twenty-Two

Praise:

Read Psalm 107:1–32 and make the psalmist's story your own, incorporating the words into your own prayer of praise.

Repent:

Turn to the Repentance section in your prayer guide. Write a prayer of repentance for any sin from the day that you need to confess and a prayer of repentance for anyone from whom you need to ask for forgiveness. With the Lord's leading, make a plan to repent to whomever it is you have sinned against.

Ask:

Turn to the appropriate day of the week in the Ask section of your prayer guide. Write a prayer for the topic you have chosen at the top of your page, using scripture to guide you in your prayers. (To find scripture to help you pray, use the tools at the back of the Ask section.)

_____

_____

_____

_____

Yield:

Turn to the Yield section in your prayer guide and write a prayer of surrender for the day, releasing your worries and anxieties and securely attaching yourself to the presence, power, and love of the Lord for all that lies ahead.

_____

_____

_____

_____

Day Twenty-Three

Praise:

Read Psalm 108:1–13 and make the psalmist's story your own, incorporating the words into your own prayer of praise.

_____

_____

_____

_____

_____

Repent:

Turn to the Repentance section in your prayer guide. Write a prayer of repentance for any sin from the day that you need to confess and a prayer confessing areas of sin and temptation with which you struggle habitually. Ask the Lord to help you guard against these sins and begin to walk out of destructive life patterns.

_____

_____

_____

_____

_____

Ask:

Turn to the appropriate day of the week in the Ask section of your prayer guide. Write a prayer for the topic you have chosen at the top of your page, using scripture to guide you in your prayers. (To find scripture to help you pray, use the tools at the back of the Ask section.)

_____

_____

_____

_____

_____

Yield:

Turn to the Yield section in your prayer guide and write a prayer of surrender for the day, releasing your worries and anxieties and securely attaching yourself to the presence, power, and love of the Lord for all that lies ahead.

_____

_____

_____

_____

_____

Day Twenty-Four

Praise:

Read Psalm 113:1–9 and make the psalmist's story your own, incorporating the words into your own prayer of praise.

_____

_____

_____

_____

Repent:

Turn to the Repentance section in your prayer guide. Write a prayer of repentance for any sin from the day that you need to confess and a prayer asking for the wisdom, accountability, and humility to see areas of past deception and temptation that could surface again and cause you to stumble and fall in the future.

_____

_____

_____

_____

Ask:

Turn to the appropriate day of the week in the Ask section of your prayer guide. Write a prayer for the topic you have chosen at the top of your page, using scripture to guide you in your prayers. (To find scripture to help you pray, use the tools at the back of the Ask section.)

_____

_____

_____

_____

Yield:

Turn to the Yield section in your prayer guide and write a prayer of surrender for the day, releasing your worries and anxieties and securely attaching yourself to the presence, power, and love of the Lord for all that lies ahead.

_____

_____

_____

_____

Day Twenty-Five

Praise:

Read Psalm 118:1–29 and make the psalmist's story your own, incorporating the words into your own prayer of praise.

_____

_____

_____

_____

Repent:

Turn to the Repentance section in your prayer guide. Write a prayer of repentance for any sin from the day that you need to confess, and then take time to pray through and receive God's forgiveness and covering love in the areas you need it the most.

_____

_____

_____

_____

Ask:

Turn to the appropriate day of the week in the Ask section of your prayer guide. Write a prayer for the topic you have chosen at the top of your page, using scripture to guide you in your prayers. (To find scripture to help you pray, use the tools at the back of the Ask section.)

_____

_____

_____

_____

_____

Yield:

Turn to the Yield section in your prayer guide and write a prayer of surrender for the day, releasing your worries and anxieties and securely attaching yourself to the presence, power, and love of the Lord for all that lies ahead.

_____

_____

_____

_____

_____

Day Twenty-Six

Praise:

Read Psalm 119:33–40 and make the psalmist's story your own, incorporating the words into your own prayer of praise.

_____

_____

_____

_____

Repent:

Turn to the Repentance section in your prayer guide. Write a prayer of repentance for any sin from the day that you need to confess and a prayer of forgiveness for those you need to forgive on a one-time or ongoing basis.

_____

_____

_____

_____

Ask:

Turn to the appropriate day of the week in the Ask section of your prayer guide. Write a prayer for the topic you have chosen at the top of your page, using scripture to guide you in your prayers. (To find scripture to help you pray, use the tools at the back of the Ask section.)

_____

_____

_____

_____

_____

Yield:

Turn to the Yield section in your prayer guide and write a prayer of surrender for the day, releasing your worries and anxieties and securely attaching yourself to the presence, power, and love of the Lord for all that lies ahead.

_____

_____

_____

_____

_____

Day Twenty-Seven

Praise:

Read Psalm 136:1–26 and make the psalmist's story your own, incorporating the words into your own prayer of praise.

_____

_____

_____

_____

_____

Repent:

Turn to the Repentance section in your prayer guide. Write a prayer of repentance for any sin from the day that you need to confess and a prayer of repentance for anyone from whom you need to ask for forgiveness. With the Lord's leading, make a plan to repent to whomever it is you have sinned against.

_____

_____

_____

_____

_____

Ask:

Turn to the appropriate day of the week in the Ask section of your prayer guide. Write a prayer for the topic you have chosen at the top of your page, using scripture to guide you in your prayers. (To find scripture to help you pray, use the tools at the back of the Ask section.)

_____

_____

_____

_____

_____

Yield:

Turn to the Yield section in your prayer guide and write a prayer of surrender for the day, releasing your worries and anxieties and securely attaching yourself to the presence, power, and love of the Lord for all that lies ahead.

_____

_____

_____

_____

_____

Day Twenty-Eight

Praise:

Read Psalm 138:1–8 and make the psalmist's story your own, incorporating the words into your own prayer of praise.

Repent:

Turn to the Repentance section in your prayer guide. Write a prayer of repentance for any sin from the day that you need to confess and a prayer confessing areas of sin and temptation with which you struggle habitually. Ask the Lord to help you guard against these sins and begin to walk out of destructive life patterns.

Ask:

Turn to the appropriate day of the week in the Ask section of your prayer guide. Write a prayer for the topic you have chosen at the top of your page, using scripture to guide you in your prayers. (To find scripture to help you pray, use the tools at the back of the Ask section.)

_____

_____

_____

_____

_____

Yield:

Turn to the Yield section in your prayer guide and write a prayer of surrender for the day, releasing your worries and anxieties and securely attaching yourself to the presence, power, and love of the Lord for all that lies ahead.

_____

_____

_____

_____

_____

Day Twenty-Nine

Praise:

Read Psalm 147:1–20 and make the psalmist's story your own, incorporating the words into your own prayer of praise.

Repent:

Turn to the Repentance section in your prayer guide. Write a prayer of repentance for any sin from the day that you need to confess and a prayer asking for the wisdom, accountability, and humility to see areas of past deception and temptation that could surface again and cause you to stumble and fall in the future.

Ask:

Turn to the appropriate day of the week in the Ask section of your prayer guide. Write a prayer for the topic you have chosen at the top of your page, using scripture to guide you in your prayers. (To find scripture to help you pray, use the tools at the back of the Ask section.)

_____

_____

_____

_____

_____

Yield:

Turn to the Yield section in your prayer guide and write a prayer of surrender for the day, releasing your worries and anxieties and securely attaching yourself to the presence, power, and love of the Lord for all that lies ahead.

_____

_____

_____

_____

_____

Day Thirty

Praise:

Read Psalm 149:1–9 and make the psalmist's story your own, incorporating the words into your own prayer of praise.

Repent:

Turn to the Repentance section in your prayer guide. Write a prayer of repentance for any sin from the day that you need to confess, and then take time to pray through and receive God's forgiveness and covering love in the areas you need it the most.

Ask:

Turn to the appropriate day of the week in the Ask section of your prayer guide. Write a prayer for the topic you have chosen at the top of your page, using scripture to guide you in your prayers. (To find scripture to help you pray, use the tools at the back of the Ask section.)

_____

_____

_____

_____

Yield:

Turn to the Yield section in your prayer guide and write a prayer of surrender for the day, releasing your worries and anxieties and securely attaching yourself to the presence, power, and love of the Lord for all that lies ahead.

_____

_____

_____

_____

Day Thirty-One

Praise:

Read Psalm 150:1–6 and make the psalmist's story your own, incorporating the words into your own prayer of praise.

_____
_____
_____
_____

Repent:

Turn to the Repentance section in your prayer guide. Write a prayer of repentance for any sin from the day that you need to confess, and then thank Him for His covering love and promise to keep your heart close to His through conviction of sin and the cleansing work of His Spirit in the days ahead.

_____
_____
_____
_____

Ask:

Turn to the appropriate day of the week in the Ask section of your prayer guide. Write a prayer for the topic you have chosen at the top of your page, using scripture to guide you in your prayers. (To find scripture to help you pray, use the tools at the back of the Ask section.)

_____

_____

_____

_____

_____

Yield:

Turn to the Yield section in your prayer guide and write a prayer of surrender for today and the days ahead. Ask God for the grace to continue in the habit of persistent prayer you have begun, securely attaching yourself to His presence and love, trusting in His provision for the days ahead.

_____

_____

_____

_____

SECURE

DON'T FORGET TO PURCHASE THE VIDEO SESSIONS FOR GROUP USE OR DOWNLOAD THE AUDIO SESSIONS **FOR FREE** WITH COUPON BELOW.

JUST FOLLOW THESE EASY STEPS.

1. Go to http://susannahbaker.com/shop/
2. Use coupon code secure1 at checkout
3. Enjoy in companion with *Secure* guide and journal

Don't forget to sign up for Susannah's email newsletter to get your free copy of her ebook *Known*, and never miss a blog post or product announcement.

www.ingramcontent.com/pod-product-compliance
Lightning Source LLC
LaVergne TN
LVHW010305070426
835507LV00027B/3447